Cambridge **Discovery Education**™
▶ **INTERACTIVE READERS**

Series editor: Bob Hastings

AVALANCHE!

B2+

Caroline Shackleton and Nathan Paul Turner

CAMBRIDGE UNIVERSITY PRESS
Cambridge, New York, Melbourne, Madrid, Cape Town,
Singapore, São Paulo, Delhi, Mexico City

Cambridge University Press
32 Avenue of the Americas, New York, NY 10013-2473, USA

www.cambridge.org
Information on this title: www.cambridge.org/9781107621572

First published 2014
Reprinted 2014

Printed in Hong Kong, China, by Golden Cup Printing Company Limited

A catalog record for this publication is available from the British Library.

Library of Congress Cataloging-in-Publication Data

Shackleton, Caroline.
  Avalanche : level B2+ / Caroline Shackleton and Nathan Paul Turner.
    pages cm. -- (Cambridge discovery interactive readers)
  ISBN 978-1-107-62157-2 (paperback : alkaline paper)
  1. Avalanches--Juvenile literature. 2. Readers (Elementary) 3. English language--Textbooks for
foreign speakers. I. Turner, Nathan Paul. II. Title.

QC929.A8S53 2014
363.34--dc23

                              20130137055

ISBN 978-1-107-62157-2

Additional resources for this publication at www.cambridge.org

Layout services, art direction, book design, and photo research: Q2ABillSMITH GROUP
Editorial services: Hyphen S.A.
Audio production: CityVox, New York
Video production: Q2ABillSMITH GROUP

Contents

Before You Read:
Get Ready!

Avalanches cause terrible damage as well as loss of life. This century, avalanches are on the increase. You will read about one of history's worst avalanche disasters, learn what causes avalanches, and find out how they can be predicted and prevented. More importantly, you will learn how to survive an avalanche.

Words to Know

Complete the definitions with the correct words.

   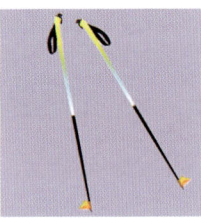

snowplow   blizzard   piste   ski poles

❶ _____ : an area of snow that has been specially prepared for skiing on

❷ _____ : a heavy machine used to clear deep snow

❸ _____ : long sticks made of wood or metal that are used for skiing

❹ _____ : storm with strong winds and snow

Words to Know

Read the sentences. Then complete the definitions with the correct highlighted words.

- After the avalanche covered the train with snow, some people were evacuated to a nearby hotel.

- 90 percent of avalanches are triggered by skiers.

- Normally, snow only builds up to form avalanches in stormy conditions.

- If you get covered by snow in an avalanche, the first thing you need to do is try to find your way to the surface.

- A snowpack is a series of layers of snow that form a large body of snow.

1 _____ : the outer or top part of something

2 _____ : caused something to start

3 _____ : increases in quantity

4 _____ : removed from a dangerous place

5 _____ : thin sheets of something, like snow or ice

?

EVALUATE

Decide whether the sentences above are true or false and check your answers as you read the story.

5

CHAPTER 1

The Worst Avalanche in US History

IN THE COLD WINTER OF 1910, TRAINS RUNNING THROUGH THE CASCADE MOUNTAINS IN WASHINGTON STATE WERE AT RISK OF ACCIDENTS. DEEP SNOW FELL ON THE TRACKS . . .

By February 21, snow was falling so heavily that it threatened to block the train lines. Managers of the Great Northern Railway Company were sent out to examine the situation. No one imagined the storms could last much longer, so the company decided the No. 25 passenger train and the No. 27 mail train could continue their journeys. They believed their snowplows would keep the lines clear.

However, a snowslide had already blocked the lines at Stevens Pass. On February 23, the two trains were stuck. The trains had no dining cars, so passengers ate in the Cascade Station dining hall with the workers. The snowplows tried unsuccessfully to clear the snow. The next day, the trains were moved to the larger town of Wellington.

The delay made some passengers nervous, but things got worse. An avalanche hit the kitchen and dining hall in Cascade. The cooks who had served the passengers were killed instantly. When the passengers heard about the disaster, some asked to be moved from the train to a safer location, but the town hotel was full.

Snow fell all weekend, trapping the trains. There were several more avalanches. In fear of their lives, some passengers left the train and walked down the mountain to a safer place.

On February 28, a railroad employee, Joseph Pettit, led another group of passengers down the mountain. Unfortunately, the telegraph[1] was out of action, so the remaining passengers could not be contacted. By the time Pettit returned, it was too late for them to leave.

Then the storm changed. Snow was replaced by wind and rain – a perfect recipe for avalanches. At 1 a.m. on March 1, lightning hit a slab[2] of snow above Wellington. A huge wall of snow started slipping down the hill towards the trains, which were full of sleeping passengers. Narrowly missing the town and its hotel, the avalanche struck the trains so hard that it threw them both nearly 50 meters down the mountain. Both trains were destroyed.

[1]**telegraph:** an old method of sending messages by electric signals
[2]**slab:** a thick, flat piece of something

People rushed to the crash site to look for survivors. A few people had been thrown clear of the rail cars and the snow. Others were found buried and were dug out. Newspapers reported that 96 people were killed – 35 passengers, including eight children, and 61 railroad employees, including Joseph Pettit. Many of the dead were not recovered until the snow melted. Only 23 passengers survived.

In an effort to forget the disaster, Wellington was renamed Tye. Later, a tunnel was built to take trains along a safer route, away from Wellington. But without the business the railroad brought into town, the people of Wellington soon left. Even though the town no longer exists, the Wellington Railway Disaster remains a disturbing reminder of the deadly power of snow.

Video Quest

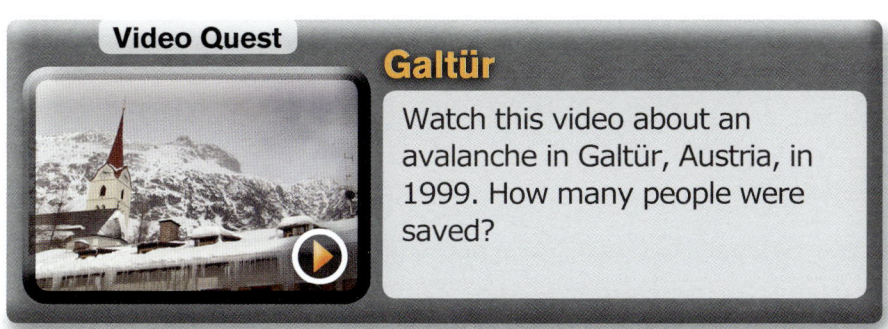

Galtür

Watch this video about an avalanche in Galtür, Austria, in 1999. How many people were saved?

CHAPTER 2

What Is an Avalanche?

AN AVALANCHE IS A SUDDEN, LARGE FALL OF SNOW DOWN A MOUNTAIN SLOPE.

There are different types of avalanches, but they are always caused by external triggers, whether man-made or natural.

Geographical Causes

The formation of an avalanche depends on several things. The angle[3] of the slope, for example, must be flat enough to allow heavy snow to form, but steep enough for the avalanche to increase speed once it is moving.

[3]**angle:** the space measured in degrees between two surfaces from the point where they meet

This is called the angle of repose, and it varies depending on the type of snowflake[4] that has fallen. Colder, drier snow needs a shallower slope, whereas warm, wet snow can stick to very steep surfaces. Most avalanches form between an angle of 25 and 60 degrees.

Weather Conditions

Weather plays a big role. Snow and rain increase the risk of an avalanche. Heavy **blizzards** add a large weight of fresh snow to the existing snow and can cause large pieces to break off. Rainstorms add to the weight of the water. They also weaken the existing layers as the rainwater sinks through the snow. The **combination** of sun and rain can cause thin layers of ice, called crusts, to form between the other layers. These crusts stop the snow layers from bonding,[5] and this makes an avalanche more likely.

[4]**snowflake:** a single piece of snow that falls from the sky
[5]**bond:** stick together

Any wind stronger than a breeze can blow snow from one area to another, causing a buildup of snow, even if it is not snowing. This buildup of snow can cause weaker layers below to break and trigger an avalanche. Wind also affects the distribution of falling snow. No wind means an even distribution, whereas strong wind can cause dangerous buildups. The stronger the wind, the more dangerous the conditions, and a moderate[6] wind on the lower slopes of a resort is much stronger at higher **altitudes**.

Types of Avalanches

There are two main types of avalanches: loose snow avalanches and slab avalanches. These are divided into wet snow and dry snow types. Loose snow avalanches happen where the snow is not as solid, either because it is fresh or because it has been warmed in the sun. They are mostly triggered by rain or melting snow, but they can also break away under the weight of skiers.

[6]**moderate:** average in size or amount and not too much

Although they rarely trap people and are not considered to be highly dangerous, larger loose snow avalanches can destroy buildings and carry people off, sometimes burying them. Loose snow avalanches can also trigger slab avalanches.

Slab avalanches are the most dangerous type and cause 90 percent of all avalanche deaths. They take place when a single large piece of solid snow, called a slab, breaks off from a larger area known as a **snowpack.** The weight of this snow causes it to fall at high speeds. In the case of hard, dry snow slabs, these speeds can reach 300 kph.

Slab avalanches are often triggered by the weight of a person moving across the snowpack. Soft, wet slab avalanches often break under the victim's feet, whereas hard, dry slab avalanches normally break higher up, leaving little chance of escape. For this reason, they are considered the more dangerous of the two.

Snowpack Formation

A snowpack is layers of snow that build up on top of each other to form a large body of snow. Each layer is different, depending on the weather when the snow fell. Snow layers may be wetter and stickier, drier and looser, or even icier and weaker. For a slab avalanche to happen, there must be one or more layers of solid snow on top of a layer of weaker snow.

Snowpacks are caused by the melting and re-freezing of snow layers when temperatures are around zero degrees Celsius. On sunny days, when temperatures may rise suddenly, melting layers in the snowpack can weaken, causing an avalanche. On the other hand, if the surface temperature of the snow is much colder than the ground level temperature, ice crystals[7] form and weaken the snowpack. Research shows that ice crystals also signal the presence of air pockets. This is a problem as it means that there is nothing holding the different layers of snow together.

[7]**ice crystal:** a small piece of ice formed together

Avalanche Fact and Myth

Despite what you might have read or seen in the movies, the one thing that will not cause an avalanche is noise. Unless it is a very loud, nearby explosion, noise rarely has the necessary strength to trigger a snowfall – though the pressure[8] from the person making the noise might!

In fact, human involvement can cause avalanches; they are sometimes caused by skiers, hikers, or climbers. The increase in popularity of winter sports has led to an increase in the number of avalanches throughout the world, especially in Europe, Canada, and the US.

....

[8] **pressure:** the force a person puts on something when they push down on it

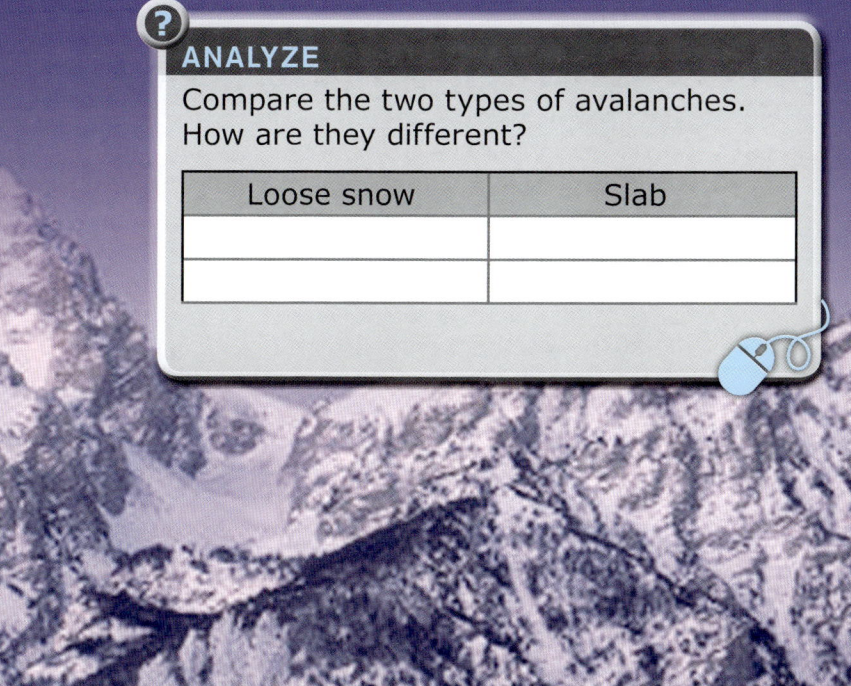

? **ANALYZE**

Compare the two types of avalanches. How are they different?

Loose snow	Slab

CHAPTER 3

Swept Away!

THE FIRST SIGN OF AN AVALANCHE IS USUALLY WHEN YOU FEEL THE GROUND SHAKE.

The next thing you know is that a raging[9] blizzard has filled the air with snow. It throws you down the mountain and buries you hundreds of meters from where you were before.

If you encounter an avalanche, try to move away to one side, or get above the line of the falling snow. If you are trapped under the snowfall, your chances of survival are just 35 percent after 30 minutes. Broken bones, organ[10] damage, shock, lack of oxygen, and extreme cold all reduce your chances of survival.

[9] **raging:** extreme
[10] **organ:** a part of the body, such as the heart or liver

If you are conscious, try to get air. One way of finding the surface is to see which way your saliva[11] falls. Next, dig an air hole by breaking through the covering snow. This is normally only possible immediately after the avalanche, as your breath will cause the snow to turn to ice. The new ice and the weight of the snow make it almost impossible to get out without help. To save oxygen and energy, stay calm. Breathe slowly and do not move around more than necessary to dig. Don't shout unless you hear people near you, as this will use up your air.

If you see someone swept away by an avalanche, try to keep visual contact with the person for as long as possible. You must find the victim quickly. Look for clues, such as gloves, skis, or boots, and use a probe[12] or a ski pole to try to find the person.

[11]**saliva:** the natural, watery liquid in the mouth
[12]**probe:** a tool used to search inside something

Most avalanche survivors owe their lives to two things: the fast reactions of their companions, and the necessary safety equipment. Traditionally, people carried avalanche probes – short metal poles that join to make one longer pole capable of reaching below the surface of the snow. Some mountaineers used to wear avalanche cords – 15-meter-long red-colored lines that dragged behind them. The lightweight lines were supposed to lie on the surface of the snow and indicate the victim's location. However, tests showed that the cords came to the surface just 40 percent of the time. Unless they had specially-trained sniffer dogs to help them, rescuers using only traditional avalanche probes often had no idea where the victim was.

Nowadays, people carry digital devices[13] called avalanche beacon-transceivers. These can be used to send a signal for others to find, or to locate another beacon-transceiver's signal. The beacon should be set to "transmit";[14] only when someone is lost should rescuers switch the beacons to "locate."

[13]**device:** a machine invented for a particular purpose
[14]**transmit:** send out a signal

Tragically, some people have died because their beacon was on the wrong setting. Another option, the passive beacon system, is put inside clothing and can be found by rescue teams using a special transmitter.

Once you locate the person, use shovels[15] to dig them out. It is essential to evacuate the victim quickly. Many people have died from cold or shock even after having been dug out.

Avalanche survival is a mixture of preparation, teamwork, suitable equipment, and lots of luck.

....

[15]**shovel:** a tool used for digging

Video Quest

Avalanche Research Test

Watch this video to find out how the team makes the rescue operation realistic. What measures do they take?

CHAPTER 4

Avoiding Avalanches

THE SUREST WAY TO SURVIVE AN AVALANCHE IS TO AVOID AN AVALANCHE.

As we have already seen, there is often very little chance of survival for anybody who is unlucky enough to be caught in an avalanche. When dealing with the destructive power of snow, the only sure method of survival is avoiding an accident in the first place. That means paying attention to avalanche warnings, traveling in groups, and carrying the appropriate equipment.

In areas of high avalanche risk, the prevention and control of avalanches has always been a top **priority**. Thankfully, researchers are continually learning more about how avalanches are formed and triggered. They are also becoming increasingly aware of the conditions that are likely to encourage snowpack formation and snowfall. This knowledge is helping scientists to develop ways of preventing further disasters.

Calculating Risk

The first thing scientists will do in an area where there is a danger of avalanches is investigate the area to calculate the level of risk. The investigation looks at the geography of the area and analyzes the typical snow formation. This allows scientists to identify places that are at risk of destruction, such as buildings, roads, or ski slopes.

When developing local evacuation plans, it is important to know where an avalanche may fall and to work out its path down the mountain. Unfortunately, there is no single way of deciding whether an avalanche is likely. Observers must use a combination of local weather information and knowledge of the mountain conditions in the area in order to try to predict the risk of an avalanche. Although it might sound obvious, the clearest sign that an area is at risk is evidence of recent avalanches!

Both scientists and skiers should constantly be aware of warning signs. For skiers, these include such things as recent snow movement, wind blowing snow across slopes, or "breaking" noises as they move through the snow.

A more precise way to learn about snow conditions is to check the different layers in a snowpack in order to look for weaknesses. To do this, scientists dig a snow pit – a deep hole in the snowpack that goes all the way down to ground level and is several meters wide.

The open face of the snow pit will show scientists the different layers of snow that have built up. By checking and comparing the hardness of each layer, scientists can see how tight the snowpack is, and this allows them to calculate the possibilities of an avalanche taking place.

Sometimes a special test called a Rutschblock test can be used to give real-life evidence. In this test, a block of snow is partially dug out from the snowpack, and a person repeatedly jumps up and down on it. This tests the ability of the block to support the actual body weight of a skier or hiker. If the block breaks on first contact, the snowpack is considered extremely risky. If it doesn't break easily, the snowpack can be considered less likely to present an immediate danger.

Types of Avalanche Control

Avalanche control is often defined as being either active or passive. Active control concentrates on strengthening the snowpack and preventing it from building up to dangerous levels. On the flatter resort pistes, this is generally done using a type of snowplow, called a snow-groomer, which repeatedly flattens the snow layers on a slope to make them safer. On steeper slopes above ski resorts, **ski patrols** sometimes use explosions to trigger smaller, controlled avalanches, either before the beginning of the tourist season, or after having evacuated the area. By triggering these smaller avalanches, the resorts are able to prevent the snow from building up and becoming a danger to skiers and mountaineers.

Passive methods try to control and redirect the flow of falling snow. This may include the planting of trees to protect slopes, or the installation of snow fences and nets to support and hold back the snow on steeper slopes. Avalanche sheds, which are concrete or metal frames, can also be used to give extra protection to any buildings or roads that are at risk.

Awareness

The combination of prevention and control methods used in ski resorts means that for the average on-piste skier, the chances of experiencing an avalanche are unlikely. However, for the off-piste skier or climber, things are very different, as avalanche prevention teams cannot stop snow buildup in more remote areas. For these more adventurous people, awareness remains the most important safety measure, and paying attention to avalanche warnings is still the best way to stay safe.

In Canada and the United States, the warning system is color-coded in order of risk, and goes from low-risk green, through yellow, orange, and red, to the highest risk level, black. Avalanche centers and ski resorts regularly publish these warnings. You should always check the avalanche warnings before a trip, because, as one avalanche expert put it, "one sign of danger beats a hundred signs of safety!"

Video Quest

Avalanche Defenses

Watch this video to learn how the ski patrol triggers avalanches. What do they do?

After You Read

Read the following questions and choose Ⓐ, Ⓑ, Ⓒ, or Ⓓ.

1 Why were the trains allowed to go into such a dangerous situation?
- Ⓐ Management made a bad decision.
- Ⓑ They had to follow the snowplows.
- Ⓒ The weather was getting much better.
- Ⓓ They couldn't find a safe place to stop.

2 Why couldn't the train passengers go to the hotel in Wellington?
- Ⓐ It was raining too hard to leave the train.
- Ⓑ They thought the train would reach its destination.
- Ⓒ There wasn't any room in the hotel.
- Ⓓ They couldn't afford to pay for the hotel.

3 What affects how quickly avalanches build up speed?
- Ⓐ how heavy they are
- Ⓑ how bad the weather is
- Ⓒ how strong the winds are
- Ⓓ how rocky the ground is

4 Which of the following is least likely to trigger an avalanche?
- Ⓐ heavy snow
- Ⓑ loud sounds
- Ⓒ warm weather
- Ⓓ light winds

5 What are the initial signs of an avalanche for most people?
- Ⓐ seeing the snow break
- Ⓑ feeling a rush of cold air
- Ⓒ a strange whistling noise
- Ⓓ a movement beneath them

6 What is the most important thing to do if you are trapped under snow?

Ⓐ Show where you are.

Ⓑ Conserve your air.

Ⓒ Move onto your side.

Ⓓ Stop ice from forming.

7 What is the most important thing for finding a victim in time?

Ⓐ calling the emergency services

Ⓑ working in large groups

Ⓒ using the right equipment

Ⓓ being in good physical condition

8 Why are off-piste skiers more at risk?

Ⓐ They don't follow official warnings.

Ⓑ They ski much more dangerously.

Ⓒ They travel in less controlled places.

Ⓓ They don't carry enough equipment.

?

ANALYZE

Think of the two most important things to remember for each category in the table below. Write an article with advice for snowboarders and skiers.

Equipment to carry with you when going into an avalanche zone	Things to do to avoid an avalanche	Things to do in the event of an avalanche
1	1	1
2	2	2

Answer Key

Words to Know, page 4
1 piste **2** snowplow **3** ski poles **4** blizzard

Words to Know, page 5
1 surface **2** triggered **3** builds up **4** evacuated
5 layers

Evaluate, page 5
false, false, false, true, true

Video Quest, page 9
26 people were saved.

Analyze, page 15

Loose snow	Slab
triggered naturally by rain or melting snow	take place when a single piece of snow, called a slab, breaks off from a larger area of solid snow, known as a snowpack
rarely trap people and are not usually seen as highly dangerous	by far the most dangerous type of avalanche, and account for 90 percent of all avalanche deaths

Video Quest, page 19
They use life-like dummies. Each dummy weighs the same as an average man. To add realism, they have snowboards.

Video Quest, page 25
They use explosives on dangerous areas of snow.

Choose the Correct Answers, page 26
1 A **2** C **3** A **4** B **5** D **6** B **7** C **8** C

Analyze, page 27
Answers will vary.